Preface

Sourdough is usually associated with the old west and early settlers but it actually goes back much earlier. Archaeologists have dated it back 6000 years to ancient Egypt.

Sourdough was a valuable item to early American settlers. Without it their limited diet could not even be livened up with hot sourdough rolls, biscuits, or pancakes.

Different sourdough starters carry different flavors and settlers used to go to great lengths to get a particular start. This start dates back to the gold rush days in Alaska. It's been passed down many generations and traveled many miles.

Moses told the sons of Israel not to eat anything with yeast in it during the week following the Passover. This included all things that are preserved with yeast.

Moses also made the one law known. The one law; not to consume blood. This means not to consume the life of another creature, i.e. genetics. This includes eggs, dairy products, sperm and blood. If you consume the genetics of another creature, you become responsible for that creature's actions. This cookbook contains no blood or animal fats. It is Kosher.

SCRUMPTIOUS SOURDOUGH

By Clint D. Knix

Copyright 1983
Revised Edition 1992

ISBN: 0-940705-00-1
SHALOM

SCRUMPTIOUS SOURDOUGH
3605 Arctic Blvd., Suite 2149
Anchorage, AK 99517

INDEX

Care of Your Sourdough 4
Sourdough Bread Sticks 5
Sourdough French Bread 6
True French Bread 7
White Bread 8
Honey Gold Bread.. 9
Rye Bread... 10
Dill Bread... 11
Bread Machine Sourdough.. 12

EGG EQUIVALENT
(equals 1 egg)

1/2 teaspoon potato starch
1/2 teaspoon corn starch
1/2 teaspoon tapioca flour
5 teaspoons water
1 teaspoon oil

Mix ingredients and whisk well before adding to recipe. Oil is optional, but if you omit it, you must add a teaspoon of water.

The reason for egg in a recipe is to make the dough very sticky. It's used in pastry and cake where low gluten flour is used. Tofu may be used as a replacer for eggs. The amounts are on the package.

SOURDOUGH GINGER COOKIES

1 cup starter
1/2 cup olive oil
1/4 cup molasses
1 egg equivalent (see egg equivalent recipe)
1 cup brown sugar
1/4 teaspoon cinnamon
1 1/2 teaspoon ginger
1 teaspoon soda
2 cups flour
1 cup powdered sugar

Cream oil, brown sugar, egg equivalent, and molasses. Stir in starter. Sift flour, soda, and spices into creamed mixture. Blend well. Chill 2 hours. Roll small ball of dough in your hand. Dip half in powdered sugar. Set sugar side up on cookie sheet. Flatten slightly.

Bake 15 minutes in 350 degree oven.

INDEX (Continued)

Zucchini Bread	13
Banana Bread	14
Cherry Nut Braid	15
Corn Bread	16
Sourdough Dinner Rolls	17
Biscuits	18
Cinnamon Rolls	19
Oatmeal Muffins	20
Blueberry Muffins	21
Pancakes	22
Blueberry Pancakes	23
Waffles	24
Popovers	25
Crepes	26
Donuts	27
Dumplings	28
Pizza Crust	29
Pie Crust	30
Dutch Oven Pie	31
Cobbler	32
Fruit Cake	33
Pecan Cake	34
Coffee Cake	35
Applesauce Cake	36
Chocolate Cake	37
White Cake	38
Carrot Cake	39
Brownies	40
Peanut Butter Brownies	41
Oatmeal Cookies	42
Spice Nut Cookies	43
Carrot Cookies	44
Chocolate Chip Cookies	45
Fruit Cookies	46
Ginger Cookies	47
Egg Equivalent	48

CARE OF SOURDOUGH

Your sourdough should be kept in a crock or glass container large enough to allow the starter to expand as it works. Never store the sourdough in a metal container or leave a metal spoon in the starter. Do not cover the container with a tight fitting lid.

To increase your sourdough or replenish it, mix equal parts of water and flour and let it sit at room temperature. If you want to store your sourdough for a long period, it can be frozen. Just remove from freezer and let thaw at room temperature for a couple of days. Your sourdough is better the more you use it. It should be used at least once a week.

Your sourdough should have a pleasant sour smell. If it smells bad, you can remove most of the starter and add fresh liquid and flour and let it work. It may form a layer of liquid on the top. It is normal. Just stir it back in the starter and add fresh flour and water. Your sourdough will work best if it has been fed within 24 hours of being used in a recipe.

For making bread a hard winter wheat with a high gluten content is essential.

This sourdough start may be used with whole wheat. Care must be taken to feed the sourdough daily when using whole wheat. The wheat germ will rot rather than be consumed by the yeast. This is the only difference in whole wheat and white.

When baking with whole wheat, about 10% more liquid is needed and a kneading time double that of white because the gluten has to become stickier to include the bran and wheat germ.

SOURDOUGH BREAD STICKS

1 cup starter
1/2 cup water
1 teaspoon yeast
2 teaspoons salt
6 cloves garlic, minced
2 - 3 cups flour

Stir starter, water, yeast, salt and garlic together in bowl. Stir in 1 cup of flour. Begin adding flour until dough is smooth and elastic. Knead well on lightly floured surface. Put in oiled bowl, cover and place in warm place to rise. When doubled, punch dough down and knead again. Pinch off small pieces and roll into ropes approximately 6 inches in length. Make them as thick or thin as you wish, but they should be all the same. Dampen them slightly and roll in sesame seeds and place on a cookie sheet lightly covered with corn meal. Let rise in warm area approximately 30 minutes.

Bake in 450 degree oven 12 - 15 minutes or until golden brown.

SCRUMPTIOUS SOURDOUGH FRENCH BREAD

2 cups starter
2 cups warm water
1 Tablespoon yeast
1 Tablespoon salt
4 to 5 cups flour

In a large mixing bowl combine starter, water, yeast and salt. Begin adding flour until dough is manageable. Knead well on a lightly floured surface. Place in bowl and set in a warm place. Let dough rise until double. Punch down and knead. Form into two long loaves and lay on a cookie sheet with a light coating of cornmeal. Lightly cut top of loaves with about 4 crosswise slashes. Spray dough with a salt water solution. Place in a warm area.

When dough is doubled, put in 500 degree oven and spray with salt water solution. After about 7 - 10 minutes, spray again with salt water solution and bake approximately 10 more minutes. When browned, remove from oven and cool on a wire rack.

TRUE SOURDOUGH FRENCH BREAD

2 cups starter
2 cups warm water
1 Tablespoon salt
4 - 5 cups flour

Mix starter, water and salt in a large mixing bowl. Begin adding flour until dough is manageable. Knead well on a floured surface. Put dough back in bowl and place in a warm area. Let dough rise until double. Punch dough down and knead. Form into 2 French loaves. Lightly cut 3 to 4 crosswise slits and spray with a 10% salt water solution. Place in warm area to rise.

When double, put in a 500 degree oven and spray again with salt water. When it starts to brown, spray again with salt water. Bake approximately 20 minutes or until browned. Remove from oven and cool on a wire rack.

SOURDOUGH WHITE BREAD

3 cups starter
3/4 cup water
2 Tablespoons olive oil
2 Tablespoons maple syrup
1 package yeast
2 teaspoons salt
4 - 5 cups white flour

Combine water, maple syrup and oil. Mix yeast, salt, and 4 cups flour in a large bowl. Add liquid mixture and starter. Stir well. Add flour as needed until dough is manageable. Knead on floured board until dough is smooth. Place dough in oiled bowl, turning so all sides are oiled. Cover bowl and let rise until double, approximately 1 hour. Punch down and allow to double again. Punch down and form into loaves. Place in oiled loaf pans and allow to double.

Bake in oven at 375 degrees for 45 - 50 minutes. Turn out on racks to cool and brush top with 10% salt water solution.

SOURDOUGH HONEY GOLD BREAD

2 cups starter
2 Tablespoons oil
1/3 cup molasses
1 teaspoon salt
1 package yeast
2 1/2 - 3 cups white flour
1 - 1 1/2 cups wheat flour

Mix together starter, oil, molasses, yeast, and salt. Add flour and beat until smooth. Cover and let stand in warm place until doubled in size. Punch down and put in oiled pan and let double again.

Bake in oven at 375 degrees until golden and it sounds hollow when you tap it.

SOURDOUGH RYE BREAD

4 cups starter
1/2 cup molasses
3 Tablespoons olive oil
1/2 cup water
1 1/2 teaspoons salt
3 cups rye flour
2 cups white flour
2 teaspoons soda
2 Tablespoons cornstarch

Mix starter, molasses, oil, cornstarch, water, and salt. Add 1 cup of rye flour and soda to starter and blend well. Add the remaining flour and knead on floured board until smooth. Roll smooth ball of dough in oiled bowl and set in a warm place, covering bowl, to raise. Let rise 2 1/2 - 3 hours. Divide dough into halves and form loaves. Place them in oiled loaf pans and roll so all sides are oiled. Cover lightly and let rise 1 1/2 hours.

Bake in 375 degree oven for 45 minutes.

SOURDOUGH DILL BREAD

2 cups starter
1/4 cup brown sugar
1 teaspoon soda
1/2 teaspoon salt
3 Tablespoons olive oil
3 - 4 cups flour
1 teaspoon dill, finely ground
10 cloves garlic, minced

Blend the starter, garlic, and oil. Add 1 cup flour, sugar, soda, salt, and dill to the starter. Mix well. Add 2 more cups flour. Add flour as needed until dough is manageable. Turn onto floured board and knead lightly. Place smooth ball of dough in oiled bowl and set in a warm place to rise. Let rise until doubled. Punch it down and divide in half. Place each half in an oiled loaf pan. Turn so all sides are oiled. Cover and let raise until doubled.

Bake 45 minutes at 375 degrees.

BREAD MACHINE SOURDOUGH

1 1/2 cups starter
1 1/2 cups flour
1 Tablespoon sugar
1 teaspoon salt
1 Tablespoon oil
1 teaspoon yeast

Pour ingredients in machine. Let rise 30 - 45 minutes. Bake at 350 degrees for 20 - 28 minutes, depending on thickness.

All the bread recipes in this book will work fine in your machine. You may have to change the proportions according to the capacity of your machine.

SOURDOUGH ZUCCHINI BREAD

1 cup starter
3 egg equivalents (see egg equivalent recipe)
1 cup oil
2 teaspoons vanilla
2 cups brown sugar
3 cups grated zucchini
3 cups flour
1 teaspoon soda
1/2 teaspoon salt
2 teaspoons cinnamon
1 teaspoon nutmeg
1 cup chopped nuts

Mix together brown sugar, egg equivalent, zucchini, oil, vanilla, and starter. Sift in the dry ingredients and stir well. Stir in the nuts. Oil and flour 3 loaf pans and fill each 1/2 full.

Bake 1 hour in a 350 degree oven.

SOURDOUGH BANANA BREAD

1 cup starter
1/3 cup shortening
2 egg equivalents (see egg equivalent recipe)
1 cup mashed bananas
3/4 cup sugar
2 cups flour
1 teaspoon salt
3/4 teaspoon baking powder
1/2 teaspoon soda
3/4 cup chopped walnuts

Cream together shortening and sugar. Add egg equivalent and banana and mix well. Stir in the starter. Sift flour with salt, baking powder, and soda. Add flour and walnuts to creamed mixture. Stir just enough to blend. Pour into an oiled 9 x 5 inch loaf pan.

Bake 1 hour at 350 degrees. Test by inserting toothpick in center. When it comes out clean, bread is done. Let cool 15 minutes before removing from pan.

SOURDOUGH CHERRY NUT BRAID

2 cups starter
1/2 cup olive oil
2 egg equivalents (see egg equivalent recipe)
2 1/2 cups flour
1/2 cup brown sugar
1/2 teaspoon salt
1/2 teaspoon soda
1/2 teaspoon cinnamon
1 Tablespoon grated lemon peel
1/2 cup raisins
1/2 cup candied cherries, chopped
1/2 cup slivered almonds

Cream oil, brown sugar, and egg equivalent. Add 1 cup flour, soda, salt, cinnamon, and lemon peel. Blend in the starter. Stir in almonds, raisins, and cherries. Begin adding flour to make dough manageable. Knead lightly on floured board. Divide dough into 3 equal parts. Form into 18 inch long strands. Place strands on an oiled cookie sheet and braid. Let rise in a warm place 2 hours.

Bake 1 hour in 350 degree oven.

SOURDOUGH CORN BREAD

1 1/2 cups starter
1 1/2 cups yellow corn meal
1 1/2 cups water
4 Tablespoons molasses
2 egg equivalents (see egg equivalent recipe)
1/3 cup olive oil
1/2 teaspoon salt
3/4 teaspoon soda

Mix starter, corn meal, water, egg equivalent and molasses. Add oil, salt, and soda. Stir well. Pour into an oiled 9 x 9 inch baking dish.

Bake 30 minutes at 450 degrees.

SCRUMPTIOUS SOURDOUGH DINNER ROLLS

1 cup starter
2 cups warm water
1 Tablespoon yeast
1 Tablespoon salt
2 Tablespoons sugar (white or brown)
2 Tablespoons olive oil
3 - 4 cups flour

In a large mixing bowl combine starter, water, yeast, salt, sugar and oil. Stir in 2 1/2 cups flour. Add flour 1/2 cup at a time until dough is manageable. Turn out onto a floured surface and knead well. Place dough in bowl and cover. Set in a warm place to rise. When double, punch dough down and form into rolls. Place in oiled roll pan and roll so all sides are lightly coated. Let rise until doubled.

Bake approximately 20 minutes in a 375 degree oven.

SOURDOUGH BISCUITS

1 cup starter
2 cups flour
2 egg equivalents (see egg equivalent recipe)
1/4 cup olive oil
2 teaspoons baking powder
1/4 teaspoon soda
1/4 teaspoon salt
2 Tablespoons brown sugar.

Combine all ingredients in a bowl. Mix well. Knead dough lightly on a floured board. Roll out to 1/2 inch thick. Cut with floured biscuit cutter. Roll in oil and place close together on a cookie sheet or pie tin.

Bake 15 - 20 minutes at 350 degrees.

SOURDOUGH CINNAMON ROLLS

1/2 cup starter
1 cup water
1/4 cup olive oil
2 egg equivalents (see egg equivalent recipe)
3 1/2 cups flour
4 Tablespoons brown sugar.
1/2 teaspoon soda
1 teaspoon baking powder
1/2 teaspoon salt
1/3 cup olive oil
1 cup brown sugar
1 1/2 teaspoons cinnamon
1 cup chopped walnuts
3/4 cup raisins

Mix starter, water, and 2 cups flour in a bowl, cover, and leave unrefrigerated at least 8 hours. To prepare rolls, beat the oil, sugar, and egg equivalent and add to starter. Stir in 1 1/2 cups flour, salt, soda, and baking powder. Turn onto floured board and knead until smooth. Roll dough into rectangle 8 x 18 inches. Brush entire rectangle with olive oil. Sprinkle with brown sugar, cinnamon, walnuts, and raisins. Roll dough up from the long side. Cut dough every 1 1/2 inches. Roll in olive oil and place in a 9 x 9 inch baking pan. Set in a warm place and let rise until doubled.
    Bake 40 minutes at 375 degrees.

SOURDOUGH OATMEAL MUFFINS

1 1/2 cups starter
1/2 cup oil
1 egg equivalent (see egg equivalent recipe)
1 cup flour
1/2 cup brown sugar
1 teaspoon salt
1 cup rolled oats

Mix together egg equivalent, oil, and starter. Add dry ingredients to starter mixture. Stir only enough to moisten. Batter will be lumpy. Fill oiled muffin tins 2/3 full.

Bake in 375 degree oven for 30 minutes.

SOURDOUGH BLUEBERRY MUFFINS

3/4 cup starter
1 egg equivalent (see egg equivalent recipe)
1/2 cup water
1/2 cup oil
2 cups flour
1/2 cup brown sugar
1 cup drained blueberries
1/2 teaspoon soda

Stir together starter, oil, water, and egg equivalent. Add sugar, flour, and soda and stir. Add blueberries. Drop into oiled muffin tins, filling cups 2/3 full.

Place in 375 degree oven and bake 40 - 45 minutes.

SOURDOUGH PANCAKES

1 cup starter
1 egg equivalent (see egg equivalent recipe)
2 Tablespoons olive oil
1 Tablespoon sugar (brown or white)
1/2 teaspoon salt
1/2 teaspoon soda

Mix starter, egg equivalent, and olive oil in a bowl. Add sugar, salt, and soda and mix well. Pour onto hot, lightly oiled griddle or skillet. Turn pancakes when covered with bubbles.

SOURDOUGH BLUEBERRY PANCAKES

1 1/2 cup starter
2 egg equivalents (see egg equivalent recipe)
2 Tablespoons oil
1 cup water
1 Tablespoon sugar (brown or white)
1 teaspoon salt
1 teaspoon soda
1 cup flour (white, wheat, or buckwheat)
1 cup blueberries, drained

Mix starter, egg equivalent, oil and water in a mixing bowl. Add sugar, salt, soda, and flour and mix well. Fold in blueberries. Pour batter onto hot, lightly oiled griddle or skillet.

SOURDOUGH WAFFLES

2 cups starter
1 egg equivalent (see egg equivalent recipe)
2 Tablespoons oil
1/2 teaspoon salt
1/2 teaspoon soda
1 Tablespoon sugar (brown or white)

Mix the starter, egg equivalent, and oil together in a medium mixing bowl. Add salt, soda, and sugar and mix. Pour batter onto hot waffle iron.

SOURDOUGH POPOVERS

1 1/2 cups starter
1/2 cup flour
1 Tablespoon oil
1/2 teaspoon salt
1 teaspoon soda
2 egg equivalent (see egg equivalent recipe)

Beat starter, oil, and egg equivalent with electric mixer. Add flour, salt, and soda and beat thoroughly. Oil 2 muffin tins and fill 2/3 full.

Place popovers in cold oven and heat up to 425 degrees. Bake 30 minutes or until golden brown.

Remove from oven and let stand 15 minutes.

Remove from tins and cool. Cut open and fill with your favorite filling.

SOURDOUGH CREPES

1 1/2 cups starter
3 egg equivalents (see egg equivalent recipe)
1/2 teaspoon salt
1 teaspoon soda

Mix all ingredients. Pour into shallow dish for dipping crepe pan in.

For desert crepes, add 2 teaspoons of sugar and 1/2 teaspoon cinnamon to the above recipe.

SOURDOUGH CAKE DONUTS

1 1/2 cups starter
2 egg equivalents (see egg equivalent recipe)
2 Tablespoons olive oil
1 cup sugar (brown or white)
1 teaspoon nutmeg
1 teaspoon cinnamon
1/2 teaspoon salt
1 1/2 teaspoon baking powder
4 - 5 cups flour

Mix starter, egg equivalent, and olive oil in a medium size mixing bowl. Sift dry ingredients together and add to the liquid mixture. Add flour as needed to form a soft dough. Refrigerate 30 minutes. Roll dough to 1/2 inch thick and cut with a well floured donut cutter. Let the dough rise 30 minutes. Drop into 400 degree oil.

When golden brown, remove and drain on paper towels. If desired, frost or sprinkle with powdered sugar.

SOURDOUGH DUMPLINGS

1 1/2 cups starter
1/4 cup water
1/4 cup chilled olive oil
1 cup flour
1 teaspoon soda
1 teaspoon salt

Sift flour, salt, and soda together in a medium bowl. Using a pastry blender, cut in chilled olive oil until it has the consistency of meal. Blend in the starter. Begin adding water a little at a time until the dough is soft. Drop by spoonfuls into bubbling stew. Cover pot and cook 15 minutes.

SOURDOUGH PIZZA CRUST

1 cups starter
1 cup flour
1/2 teaspoon salt
1 Tablespoon olive oil
1 teaspoon yeast (optional)

Mix all ingredients together adding four as needed to make dough smooth. Let dough rest 15 minutes in a warm place. Roll dough out and place on an oiled pizza pan.

Bake in oven at 475 degrees for 5 minutes.

Remove from oven and add sauce, and your favorite toppings. Return to oven and bake 15 - 20 minutes.

SOURDOUGH PIE CRUST

1/2 cups starter
1 1/2 cup flour
1/2 teaspoon salt
1/2 cup chilled olive oil

Sift flour and salt into a bowl. Cut in chilled olive oil with a pastry blender until crumbly. Stir in starter until dough clings together but is not sticky. Add just enough flour to make dough manageable. Roll out 1/2 dough at a time.

SOURDOUGH DUTCH OVEN PIE

1 cup starter
1 teaspoon soda
1/2 teaspoon salt
4 Tablespoons olive oil
4 Tablespoons brown sugar
1 1/2 cups sugar (brown or white)
1 teaspoon allspice
1 teaspoon nutmeg
4 Tablespoons cornstarch
2 cups berries (cherries, strawberries, blueberries, etc.)

Mix berries, cornstarch, allspice, 1 1/2 cups sugar, and nutmeg in sauce pan. Simmer on stove 5 minutes. Meanwhile, mix 4 Tablespoons brown sugar, oil, starter, soda, and salt together. Pour berries in 9 x 9 inch dish. Pour batter over berries.

Bake 40 minutes at 300 degrees. Serve warm.

SOURDOUGH COBBLER

3/4 cup starter
3/4 cup flour
1 cup sugar (brown or white)
1/2 teaspoon cinnamon
1/2 cup olive oil
1/2 cup chopped nuts
2 cups fruit pie filling

Place pie filling an oiled 8 x 8 inch baking dish. In a mixing bowl combine flour, sugar, and cinnamon. Cut in oil with pastry blender. Stir in nuts and starter. Spoon dough mixture over fruit.

Bake 25 minutes at 425 degrees.

SOURDOUGH FRUIT CAKE

1 cup starter
4 cups flour
1 teaspoon salt
1 teaspoon soda
2 egg equivalent (see egg equivalent recipe)
1/2 teaspoon allspice
1/2 teaspoon nutmeg
1 teaspoon cinnamon
2/3 cup olive oil
1 3/4 cup sugar (brown or white)
1 1/2 cup raisins
1 cup currants
3 cups fruit
1 cup apple cider
1 1/2 cups chopped nuts

Rinse raisins and currants. Put raisins, currants, fruit, and cider in covered bowl and let stand over night. Cream sugar, oil and spices until fluffy. Add egg equivalent and starter and beat. Combine fruit and nuts and add to mixture. Sift flour, salt, and soda into batter. Mix well and pour into well oiled loaf pans.

Bake 90 minutes in 300 degree oven. Remove from pans and cool. Store in the refrigerator. Makes 6 loaves.

SOURDOUGH PECAN CAKE

3/4 cup starter
1/2 cup water
1 egg equivalent (see egg equivalent recipe)
1/2 teaspoon vanilla
1/3 cup olive oil
1 cup brown sugar
1 1/2 cups flour
1 teaspoon soda
1/4 teaspoon salt

Beat olive oil, brown sugar, egg equivalent, vanilla and water until fluffy. Stir in starter. Sift flour, soda, and salt into batter. Pour into oiled 8 inch tube pan.

Bake 35 minutes at 350 degrees. Remove from pan. Glaze when cool.

GLAZE

3/4 cup water
2 Tablespoons olive oil
1/4 teaspoon salt
5 Tablespoons cornstarch
3/4 cup brown sugar

In a sauce pan combine cornstarch, brown sugar, salt, oil and water. Cook stirring constantly. Boil 1 minute. Remove from heat. Let cool. Spread over cake and cover with whole pecans.

SOURDOUGH COFFEE CAKE

1 cup starter
1/4 cup water
2 egg equivalents (see egg equivalent recipe)
1/2 cup olive oil
1 teaspoon vanilla
1 1/2 cups flour
1 teaspoon soda
1/2 teaspoon salt
1 teaspoon cocoa
1 teaspoon instant coffee
1 cup chopped nuts
1 cup brown sugar

Cream oil and sugar. Add egg equivalent and vanilla. Blend in flour, soda, salt, cocoa, and instant coffee. Add water and starter. Mix well. Stir in nuts and pour into oiled 9 x 9 inch baking dish.

Bake at 350 degrees for 45 minutes.

SOURDOUGH APPLESAUCE CAKE

1 1/2 cup starter
1 1/4 cups flour
1 cup applesauce
1 1/4 cup brown sugar
1/2 cup olive oil
2 egg equivalent (see egg equivalent recipe)
1/4 teaspoon salt
2 teaspoons soda
1 teaspoon cinnamon
1/2 teaspoon cloves
1/4 teaspoon allspice
1/2 teaspoon nutmeg
1 cup chopped nuts
1 cup raisins

Mix together starter, flour, and applesauce. In a separate bowl, mix brown sugar and oil. In another bowl, beat the egg equivalent, salt, soda, spices, nuts, and raisins. Combine all three bowls and beat well. Pour into oiled and floured baking pan 9 x 13 inches.

Bake at 350 degrees for 30 minutes.

SOURDOUGH CHOCOLATE CAKE

1 cup starter
3 egg equivalents (see egg equivalent recipe)
2 cups sugar (brown or white)
2 cups flour
2/3 cup olive oil
3/4 cup cocoa
1/2 teaspoon baking powder
1 1/2 teaspoon soda
1/2 teaspoon salt
1 teaspoon vanilla
1 cup water

Cream oil, sugar, and egg equivalent. Add starter. Mix flour, cocoa, baking powder, soda, and salt into batter. Add vanilla and water. Mix at medium speed until smooth. Pour into oiled and floured cake pans.

Bake at 375 degrees for 30 - 45 minutes depending on size of pans used. Test by pressing lightly on center of cake. If it springs back, cake is done.

SOURDOUGH WHITE CAKE

1 cup starter
1/4 cup water
1 cup olive oil
1 1/2 cup sugar
3 egg equivalents (see egg equivalent recipe)
1 teaspoon vanilla
1 1/2 cup flour
1/2 teaspoon baking powder
1/2 teaspoon soda
1/2 teaspoon salt

Cream oil and sugar. Mix in egg equivalent and vanilla. Sift dry ingredients into sugar mixture. Add starter and water. Mix at medium speed 2 minutes. Pour batter into oiled and floured cake pans.

Bake at 375 degrees for 30 - 45 minutes. Test cake by lightly touching center. If cake springs back, it's done.

SOURDOUGH CARROT CAKE

1 1/2 cups starter
1 cup flour
1 cup grated carrots
1 1/4 cup sugar (brown or white)
1/2 cup olive oil
2 egg equivalent (see egg equivalent recipe)
1 teaspoon salt
1 teaspoon soda
1 teaspoon cinnamon
1 teaspoon nutmeg
1/2 teaspoon allspice
1/2 teaspoon cloves
1/2 cup nuts
1 cup raisins

Mix together starter, egg equivalent, flour, and carrots. Combine sugar and olive oil. In a separate bowl, mix salt, soda, spices, nuts, and raisins. Mix all together and beat well. Pour into oiled and floured cake pans.

Bake 30 - 45 minutes at 350 degrees. Test cake by lightly touching center. If it springs back, it's done.

SOURDOUGH BROWNIES

1 1/2 cups starter
1 cup olive oil
4 ounces sweet cooking chocolate
1/2 cup hot water
1 1/2 teaspoons vanilla
1 teaspoon soda
2 cups sugar (brown or white)
4 egg equivalents (see egg equivalent recipe)
1 cup flour
1/2 teaspoon salt
1/2 teaspoon baking powder
1 cup chopped nuts

Place chocolate and hot water in a small pan and heat until chocolate is melted, stirring constantly. Remove from stove and stir in soda. Cream oil and sugar in mixing bow. Add the egg equivalent and mix well. Stir in vanilla and chocolate. Add the starter and mix. Blend in the flour, salt, and baking powder. Beat until smooth. Stir in nuts just enough to blend. Pour batter into 2 oiled and floured 9 x 9 inch pans.

Bake in 350 degree oven for 45 minutes.

SOURDOUGH PEANUT BUTTER BROWNIES

1 cup starter
2 egg equivalents (see egg eqivalent recipe)
1/3 cup olive oil
3/4 cup peanut butter
1 1/4 cup sugar (brown or white)
1/2 teaspoon vanilla
2 1/4 cups flour
1/4 teaspoon salt
1 teaspoon soda
1 cup chocolate chips
1/2 cup chopped nuts

Cream oil, sugar, and peanut butter. Add egg equivalent, starter and vanilla. Add the flour, salt, and soda and blend. Fold in chocolate chips and nuts. Spread batter into a 9 x 13 x 2 inch oiled pan.

Bake in 350 degree oven for 30 minutes. Cut in squares.

SOURDOUGH OATMEAL COOKIES

2 cups starter
1 cup olive oil
1 egg equivalent (see egg equivalent recipe)
1 teaspoon vanilla
1 1/2 cups sugar (brown or white)
1/2 teaspoon soda
1 teaspoon cinnamon
1/2 teaspoon salt
2 cups flour
1 1/2 cups rolled oats

Cream oil, sugar, and egg equivalent. Add the starter and vanilla and mix will. Sift in soda, flour, cinnamon, and salt. Mix well. Add rolled oats and stir. Drop by spoonfuls onto an oiled cookie sheet.

Bake 12 - 15 minutes in 400 degree oven. Yield: 4 dozen.

SOURDOUGH
SPICE NUT COOKIES

1/2 cups starter
1/4 cup olive oil
1/2 cup molasses
1 egg equivalent (see egg equivalent recipe)
1/2 cups sugar (brown or white)
2 cups flour
1/2 teaspoon salt
1 teaspoon ginger
1/2 teaspoon cinnamon
1/2 teaspoon cloves
1/2 teaspoon allspice
1 teaspoon soda
1/2 cup chopped nuts

Mix together starter, oil, molasses, egg equivalent and brown sugar. Combine the dry ingredients and add to starter mixture. Beat well. Stir in the nuts. Drop by spoonfuls onto oiled cookie sheet.

Bake 12 - 15 minutes at 375 degrees.

SOURDOUGH CARROT COOKIES

1/2 cups starter
3/4 cup olive oil
1 egg equivalent (see egg equivalent recipe)
1 teaspoon vanilla
1 cup cooked and mashed carrots
3/4 cup sugar (brown or white)
2 cups flour
1/4 teaspoon salt
1 teaspoon soda
1/2 cup raisins
1/2 cup chopped nuts

Beat oil, sugar, and egg equivalent. Stir in the carrots, starter, and vanilla. Sift the flour, soda, and salt and add to creamed mixture. Stir in the nuts and raisins. Drop by spoonfuls onto an oiled cookie sheet.

Bake in 350 degree oven for 12 - 15 minutes.

SOURDOUGH CHOCOLATE CHIP COOKIES

1 1/2 cups starter
1 cup olive oil
2 egg equivalents (see egg equivalent recipe)
1 teaspoon vanilla
1 1/2 cup sugar (brown or white)
3 teaspoons soda
1 teaspoon baking powder
3 cups flour
2 cups semi-sweet chocolate chips

Cream together oil, sugar, vanilla, and egg equivalent. Stir in the starter. Sift in flour, soda, and baking powder. Fold in the chocolate chips. Drop by spoonfuls onto an oiled cookie sheet.

Bake 10 - 12 minutes in 375 degree oven.

SOURDOUGH FRUIT COOKIES

1 cup starter
1 cup water
1 cup olive oil
1 cup brown sugar
2 cups flour
1 Tablespoon soda
2 teaspoons cinnamon
1/2 teaspoon nutmeg
2 teaspoons allspice
1 teaspoon cloves
1 cup raisins
1 cup dates
1 cup chopped nuts

In a sauce pan boil water, dates, raisins, sugar, oil, and spices for 4 minutes. Remove from heat and let cool. Add starter, flour, soda, and nuts. Blend well. Drop by spoonfuls on an oiled cookie sheet.

Bake 12 minutes at 350 degrees.